SEMINAR ON ENERGY POLICY
THE CARTER PROPOSALS

Edward J. Mitchell, editor

Morris A. Adelman
Richard L. Gordon
William W. Hogan
Milton Russell

American Enterprise Institute for Public Policy Research
Washington, D.C.

333.7
M68IS

ISBN 0-8447-3355-5

Library of Congress Catalog Card No. 79-55341

AEI Studies 252

CONTENTS

Preface

On July 16, 1979, President Carter announced energy policy proposals intended to reduce U.S. oil imports by 4½ million barrels per day by 1990. These proposals included:

- limiting net oil imports to not greater than 1977 levels
- creation of an Energy Security Corporation to direct government investment in the development of synthetic fuels over the next decade
- creation of an Energy Mobilization Board to expedite critical energy development projects
- provision of new incentives for the development of unconventional energy resources
- mandatory oil consumption reduction by utilities
- establishment of a new residential and commercial conservation program
- provision of additional financial assistance to low-income families
- new government investments in mass transportation and automobile fuel efficiency.

In response to the proposals, the American Enterprise Institute held before some forty members of the press a seminar on national energy policy issues. Energy economist participants and their prepared topics were: Morris A. Adelman (M.I.T.) on the world oil market; Richard L. Gordon (The Pennsylvania State University) on coal policy; William W. Hogan (Harvard) on conservation policy; and Milton Russell (Resources for the Future) on synthetic and alternative fuels. I discussed import quotas. Questions from the press centered on the government's potential involvement in synthetic fuels development and the desirability of import tariffs versus quotas as instruments of import reduction and price stabilization. There was some agreement among the economists that a crash synfuels program would not change the overall strategic role of oil. Further, it was predicted that such an effort would probably increase the long-run costs of synfuels. Also expressed was the view that neither tariffs nor quotas could, in the absence of domestic oil price deregulation, contribute either to national security or to the reliability of supplies. However, a tariff was seen as preferable because it would tend to lower OPEC prices, while a quota would tend to raise them.

EDWARD J. MITCHELL

Seminar on Energy Policy
The Carter Proposals

1

MILTON RUSSELL
Senior Fellow
Resources for the Future

As background today, I should mention that some of my colleagues at Resources for the Future and I, in about three weeks, will be releasing the results of a three-year study, *Energy in America's Future: The Choices Before Us,* which looks comprehensively at energy supply and conservation alternatives, including environmental, economic, and other policy questions and examines quite extensively the synthetic fuels program.

But today I am speaking for myself alone, and I am not giving a summary of those findings, partly because I do not want to be in the position of summarizing my coauthors' work. Also, of course, I ought to note that RFF, as an institution, never takes a position on such issues.

I would like to talk about three fundamental questions that ought to be addressed in a synthetic fuels program: First, what functions might a synthetic fuels program play in solving the energy problems we face? Second, what are the economic difficulties or problems in getting a program of 2.5 million barrels a day in place by 1990? And, third, what principles should guide the selection of subsidy instruments if a program is going to be pursued?

The President really has defined neither his program nor its scope, so my comments today will have to be very general. The choice of technologies and instruments in the President's program is left to the Energy Security Corporation. Expediting the program is left to the Energy Mobilization Board. The size of the program depends on the uncertain revenues of the so-called windfall profits tax.

But he certainly has enunciated a goal—a goal of 2½ million barrels a day of oil import replacement by 1990—and I will be addressing that goal.

First, let's look at the possible functions of a synthetic fuels program. It can have several goals and several different configurations, depending on which goal is emphasized. But one goal it *cannot* meet is to provide an early defense against import interruptions. The lead times are too long; the volumes are too small. But since energy insecurity is not a short-run problem, but one that will be with us perpetually, there can be some *future* security benefits from a synthetic fuels program.

A second goal could be to find out what the long-run costs of energy will be and to try to lower them. By finding out what those costs would be, we could plan better; we could make long-run adjustments easier; we could avoid the problems that businesses and all the rest of us are facing today of trying to figure out what to do when we don't know whether energy by the year 2010 will be one and a half times or three times as expensive as it is now.

A program designed to find out about the cost and practicality of producing synthetic fuels could also reduce the long-run cost of energy. It would seek to bring on—in an orderly way but faster than would occur without some government action—the most economical array of energy alternatives.

In design, such a program would investigate alternatives, concentrating first on producing information and not energy, and it would avoid a premature commitment to current generation technologies. By doing so it would put, or it could put, an earlier and perhaps lower cap on the price of imported oil.

Such a program would lessen the lags in building plants in the event of a sustained oil supply emergency, but it wouldn't promise much relief from import interruptions in the intermediate term, say, from five to fifteen years in the future. Note again, though, it could make oil exporters more cautious in their pricing and supply actions.

This is a synfuels program designed for information and earlier production of oil but not for immediate import relief.

A final goal could be to reduce import dependence as early and as significantly as possible. This appears to be the President's goal and one which is getting much support from Congress. This goal implies that the benefits from early import reduction are worth its costs, and that a crash synfuels program is the best way of achieving that reduction.

I would submit that neither of those propositions is obvious. While I would support government efforts to foster alternative fuel capability in general, there are some serious reservations about the wisdom and feasibility of some of the current proposals. A crash program probably implies a higher long-run cost of synthetic-based energy than a more orderly program and, depending on oil exporter reactions, could lead to higher, not lower, intermediate term oil costs, as well.

Keep in mind that even the most ambitious and successful crash program would not change the overall strategic role of oil. The volumes involved would be small in terms of world totals; the United States would still be dependent on some imports; we would still be concerned with the fuel supplies of our trading partners and allies abroad.

In narrow terms, a successful crash program would only give us more short-run discretion in foreign and domestic policy in the face of oil exporter actions. But, of course, those same goals could be achieved by more conventional oil and gas production, or more conservation.

Now, so much for the reasons for a program. How about achieving it? I am going to ignore here the real environmental hazards, which I think can be overcome in time and, also, the environmental procedural roadblocks which may prove very difficult to remove, even with the Energy Mobilization Board. It takes more than an executive order to put down protests if enough dedicated people feel strongly enough to act against some action.

But the economic problems are serious enough. They involve availability of top-flight managerial skills, equipment production capacity, adequate skilled labor, and, possibly, transportation capacity.

Synfuel plants are very large enterprises. A 50,000-barrel-a-day coal plant will probably cost, at a minimum, $2 billion. It uses several times as much coal as the largest electric generating plant in existence, and no one has ever built one at this scale or at a scale approaching it. And we are talking about building twenty or thirty of them in the next ten years.

Another set of plants—using essentially the same heavy construction and engineering skills, the same industrial base, the same people—will be required for the oil-shale program. And we are talking about building about ten of those in the next ten years. At the same time, we will be building coal and nuclear electric plants not only for expansion but, according to the President's program, to replace 750,000-barrels-per-day oil use—another twenty-five, perhaps, similar-sized plants there.

We do not have the unemployed managers, skilled laborers, and production equipment to utilize as we did in the era that is so often being referred to—that is, the era when war production expanded in 1941. The managers, engineers, and laborers will have to be trained, or diverted from other activities. New plants will have to be built to produce the equipment going into the synthetic fuels plants, and plants built to build the plants to build the equipment to build them.

Resource redirection and mobilization are the activities at which a free enterprise society excels, but they still take time. And before they really begin, note, the legislation must pass, the Energy Security Corporation must get organized, the types of plants have to be specified, operating firms selected, specific sites chosen (and that may prove troublesome), environmental approvals granted, and the plants designed and engineered, and then made to work at scales not previously experienced.

Some of these steps can be compressed, but, taken together, the prospects for anything like 2½ million barrels per day by 1990 seem to be slim, unless—and this is the important "unless"—unless, as a nation, we decide nothing much else is important. And the question, then, is, Does that kind of political will exist?

Some of these constraints can be lessened by importing from abroad and relying, somewhat, on the industrial capacity of Europe and Japan. In fact, I would suggest that one test of how serious we are about meeting the 2½ million-barrels-per-day goal would be whether we can avoid any restrictions on imports of skilled labor and equipment for this program. Note, though, that such imports will lessen the balance of payments benefits of reduced oil importation and create other problems, including some serious political ones.

Inevitably, the faster the program is pushed, the higher will be its cost. These costs are paid in three ways, and we ought to isolate those three kinds of costs.

First is the direct waste involved: That waste occurs when the same mistakes are made in a lot of places at once, when cheaper ways and advanced technologies are not pursued because something else may be faster, when redundant paths are followed because there is no time to learn, and when bottlenecks that show up anywhere mean that time and effort is lost everywhere. These wastes show up in higher fuel costs from the plants themselves.

The second cost is displayed in lower output in the rest of the economy as shortages and distortions show up because labor and equipment are diverted to synfuels tasks.

The third cost—one which I think deserves some very special attention—is in energy production from conventional and other sources. As capital is pulled away from conservation activities, from searching for conventional oil and gas; as equipment and labor is diverted from building coal and nuclear power plants and their production schedules slow down; as engineering and geological skills and, even, drilling equipment is diverted from searching for conventional natural gas to working on more speculative efforts to produce nonconventional gas—then there will be less production of other domestic energy.

4

This last cost should be carefully examined in evaluating even a successful program. The point is that, even if 2.5 million barrels per day were produced in a synthetic fuels program by 1990, that does not translate into an import reduction of 2.5 million barrels per day during the same time period because of the loss of energy supplies elsewhere in the economy.

The final topic I want to touch on today is appropriate subsidy instruments in the event we want to go ahead with this program. There are many alternatives. They have distinctly different effects.

I would suggest that there are three goals for those instruments, and that those goals are fairly clear. First, they should be effective in getting the output desired.

Second, those instruments should minimize costs to the economy—note, the economy not the government—per unit of extra energy produced, taking into account the loss of other energy that is not produced.

And, last, those instruments should give each operating company every incentive to be efficient, using whatever plant and equipment it ends up with.

I will identify a few principles to follow in achieving these goals but will not be specific now—we can return to this topic in the question session.

First, maximum flexibility should be allowed the private sector in choosing technologies and methods. Government should specify the output it wants to buy, not the process it wants to have used.

Second, subsidies should be arranged so that the private firm always benefits when its costs are lower and always suffers when its costs are higher. Thus, subsidies should be in the form of lump-sum or first-cost contributions and, certainly, should not take the cost-plus path.

Third, subsidies should be allocated by bid. Bidding can assure that the most effective firms and technologies are chosen. It will hold the costs down, and the fact that firms bear the risks will make those bids realistic.

Fourth, the subsidy instruments chosen should be ones that open the bidding process to the widest number of bidders. Some instruments are such as to increase the breadth of bidding; others are not, and that should be an important consideration in choosing the instruments involved.

And, last, subsidies should be directed so that economic uncertainty, which has been a serious problem in energy supply and energy conservation, should be minimized. Investors should know from day one what the subsidy will be on which they are bidding, and that there is no opportunity for the government to change its mind later. Thus, there should be no discretion for renegotiating the subsidy downward if costs turn out to be lower, or upward if they turn out to be higher than anticipated. And companies that take the risks should be assured that, if it turns out that oil prices rise much higher than anticipated, they will be able to sell their product at the world price, without price controls, and without repayment of the earlier subsidy.

In general, I guess I would conclude that synfuels programs are not *the* answer to the energy problem, and to focus on their output without considering the broad effects on the economy and even on the rest of the energy sector might be a very big mistake. But they can be *part* of the answer.

Too many appear to be jumping on a bandwagon without thinking about what tune they actually want the bandwagon to end up playing.

2

WILLIAM W. HOGAN
Professor of Political Economy
Director, Energy and Environmental Policy Center
Harvard University

Energy conservation has been the keystone of Carter policy since his inauguration, and the latest announcements do not change dramatically the structure of the conservation program; they are primarily some new wrinkles and re-emphasis of previous policies. So what I thought I would do is just comment on the cumulative effect of the conservation and demand changes and on what I see in the latest initiatives that might have an impact on the future of energy conservation.

The problem, of course, in discussing energy conservation, is that it is very diverse, and there are some difficulties in defining it. Generally speaking, as an economist, I believe that, other things being equal, when energy is inexpensive, people want more of it than they would when energy is expensive. After a period like 1973-1974, when there was a sharp increase in the costs of energy to the consumers—in the prices they had to pay—we found many people had been using more energy than would be efficient for them at these higher prices, and so the potential for conservation would be very great. In a very real sense, conservation is very inexpensive. In adjusting to these higher prices, it is cheaper not to use oil at the higher prices than to use it for something which has a value less than we have to pay for it.

I expect that this argument is not going to be accepted by everyone. It certainly is the keystone, though, of the economists' view of demand elasticities and the changes that will occur as a result of higher prices.

What actually did happen? I have summarized some of the statistics on energy demand changes in the United States between 1972 and 1978. The real price of imported oil to the United States increased 160 percent. This is a big change, but it is not quite as big as we often hear, because it is corrected for the effects of inflation.

When we look at the price that consumers pay—the aggregate energy prices to the user across oil, gas, and electricity, aggregating across the many different products and different kinds of users—we find that, over the same period, the real increase was only 30 percent, much smaller than we might believe. At the same time, we observed a change in the energy use per dollar of GNP, the energy delivered to these final consumers decreased by 12 percent. This is a nontrivial reduction in the energy utilization per dollar of GNP, which has been matched by most, if not all, other countries around the world that experienced similar increases in energy prices.

These changes are substantially smaller than many economists have argued for in the past, and most would continue to argue that they are smaller than the full adjustments that might be realized.

Comparing international statistics, we find that in 1976 West Germany paid 70 percent more than Americans for fuels and transportation and used 45 percent less than we did. At the same time, if we look at the same aggregate energy—energy delivered to the consumers—we see they paid 40 percent more than Americans and used 25 percent less.

The technological analyses we are so familiar with—those that conservation advocates support for conservation initiatives—include many examples of ways to operate industrial processes or to design appliances that use less energy per unit of output, not necessarily less cost per unit of output, but at least use less energy. These detailed analyses suggest that we might get up to a 40 percent decrease in the use of energy per unit of output in the United States.

This is a broad average of the technological analyses that have been done.

The automobile efficiency standards that we have already legislated are designed to change the new car fleet efficiency from less than 15 miles per gallon in 1975 to 27½ miles per gallon in 1985. Other things being equal, this change will reduce gasoline demand by as much as 45 percent compared with what it would have been otherwise.

These figures—40 percent, 45 percent, and so forth—are much more dramatic than the 12 percent adjustment in energy use per dollar GNP that we have seen so far. I think the explanation of the difference between those two ranges can be found in the fact that it takes time to make the adjustments.

The process of adjustment is very slow. In particular, if we think that people make their primary changes in the energy efficiency of equipment at the time of the purchase of new equipment or the construction of new buildings, then it is obvious that the complete turnover of the stock is going to take quite a while.

Following this logic—and we could look at it in more detail—we could convince ourselves fairly quickly that we have seen less than half the demand reductions expected just from current energy prices. So, even if prices did not go up any more, we would still see further reductions in energy demand per dollar GNP, with energy demand growing slower than the growth of the GNP.

With a moderate further increase of 30 percent in the delivered energy prices, the kind of increase that would occur if we just let current oil prices work through the system and allowed adjustments to take place in response to those higher prices, energy productivity, defined as the energy used per dollar of GNP, could be 30 percent better by the turn of the century than it was in 1972. This figure is somewhat smaller than the comparison of the international statistics, but it is certainly consistent with that level and consistent with the economists' argument about a large long-run potential to adjust the demand for energy, that is, a large demand elasticity.

If we take as our view on energy conservation that, other things being equal, higher prices will induce people to use less energy, we might ask how has the policy fared so far. Has it adapted to the world of higher energy prices and given the signals to consumers that energy will be more expensive and that they should change the way they use it and the kinds of equipment they use?

I think the conservation actions proposed by this administration and previous administrations are a mixed bag, reflecting the problems of getting any kind of major change through our political system. The Natural Gas Pricing Act and the eventual decontrol of natural gas prices by 1985 or 1987 for new natural gas is a step in the right direction of sending the message to the consumers, but it certainly is not what could be called excessively hasty. And there is always the possibility it will be delayed even further, particularly if we see additional increases in the price of competing fuels such as oil.

The proposed phased decontrol of crude oil prices by 1981 is another step in the right direction. President Carter has embarked upon this road. I hope he makes it. We have missed the chance a few times in the past, under other administrations, to decontrol crude oil prices. It is probably optimistic to hope that we could have instant decontrol, but I think we are moving in the right direction.

The mandatory standards for automobiles, the efficiency standards that have already been legislated, are not the kind of incentive that comes through the price system; rather this is a direct intervention by the government. Most analyses I am familiar with suggest that the efficiency standards are much more rigid than consumers would adopt on their own, given current or expected prices for gasoline. So, it may be that they are economically inefficient. They certainly will be effective, however, in reducing gasoline demand on automobiles.

The Department of Energy is trying to set mandatory standards for appliances, building efficiency performance standards, and other such mandatory procedures by which we can control the way that energy is used in this country. How successful those will be is something I'll return to in a moment.

We have the mandatory thermostat settings, which have already been enforced. We are familiar with the cartoon about the thermostat police, the large army that will be required to enforce these standards if there is widespread violation.

Also, we have PURPA. The Public Utilities Regulatory Policy Act directed the states to consider marginal cost pricing, to convey the message to consumers that electricity is expensive—and more expensive at different times of the day and different seasons of the year. This is a step in the right direction.

In regard to other programs, like the energy audits and loans by utilities, the latest Carter proposal was right in suggesting that utilities be allowed to make loans to individuals for conservation changes in their homes, and to change the legislation in the National Energy Conservation Policy Act which forbids utilities from getting into the conservation business.

And then we have things like the weatherization program, which is off to a slow start. In the long run, it may be better as an income redistribution effort, trying to change the energy consumption of low-income families, rather than providing them the money to pay for the oil they are wasting because they can't afford to weatherize their houses. But I understand the Department of Energy has succeeded so far in weatherizing only 171,000 out of a potential 14 million low-income houses. There is a long way to go here.

There are other programs, for example, the coal conversion program, and we could go on. I think the point is made that in the present policy there are few efforts to convey the message to the consumer to adjust the energy use, to conserve energy, and there are many programs to impose standards and develop mandatory controls. I am skeptical as to how successful the regulations will be.

What I am more concerned about is the main thrust of the President's latest package, which is a supply-oriented synthetic fuels proposal, and the kinds of subsidies that are developed there. Rather than carrying the message to the consumer that imported oil is expensive, at least more expensive than is indicated by the price of oil, in the view of the President, we are constructing an ever more elaborate array of subsidies, on the supply side, to compensate for the imported oil, without carrying higher prices to the consumer.

The $5-per-barrel entitlement for distillate is the most recent example; others are the $3-per-barrel tax credit for shale oil, $16.80 per barrel for ethanol to use in gasohol, and roughly the $15- to $20-per-barrel equivalent for solar investments. In round numbers, for synthetic fuels we are talking about $15- to $20-per-barrel subsidies—subsidies above the price of imported oil—that are being constructed for these many alternative supply forms. This is going to move us farther and farther away from the kinds of signals we would like to send to consumers about how much the energy they are using is really costing the economy and them, indirectly.

And the problem is compounded because it is very difficult—I believe, impossible—for the government to come close to identifying all the ways that people could conserve energy if they were confronted with these higher prices. Efficiency standards for appliances and automobiles might be the exceptions, but changes in the way the people live or the way that they drive are not easy to see. The price information, the price signals conveyed to the consumer, I believe, would be far more effective. We are going to miss many opportunities that could be there if we conveyed the proper marginal cost signals.

Another potentially serious political problem for the government —which administration, I'm not sure—depends on whether or not this mandatory quota, which we'll hear about in a moment, bites and actually does restrict oil imports before we remove price controls on crude oil. If that quota bites, and the effective prices of imported oil start going up, there will be a very strong tendency to extend, or reimpose, elaborate price controls so that the consumer doesn't have to see the sudden increases in prices that could occur with a strict import quota.

I suspect that it will be very difficult for any administration to resist this temptation, so I am hoping that we can remove the price control mechanisms before the quota starts to bite. If not, then I suspect that the hopes for decontrol by the end of 1981, or for natural gas pricing decontrol by 1985, will go the way of the hopes for earlier programs for phased decontrol. Then the conservation adjustments that we could have made, which are slow, will be delayed even further, to the loss of the economy and the consumers in general.

3

RICHARD L. GORDON
Professor of Mineral Economics
The Pennsylvania State University

It is a rather regrettable comment on the lack of progress we are making in energy policy that the article on coal policy I wrote almost a year ago, for the AEI journal *Regulation,* is still an accurate statement of the situation. Basically, President Carter's approach to coal, like most of his energy programs, involves an unfortunate combination of inconsistency and excessive complexity.

The inconsistency problem long antedates the Carter administration. For over a decade, the real thrust of public policy on the coal industry has been to impose ever-increasing restrictions on the production and use of coal. In effect, all the presidential statements about encouraging coal use thus have been empty rhetoric.

President Carter's contribution has been to increase greatly the tendency to devise complicated new programs that purport to offset the effects of existing barriers to coal production. Quite clearly, it would be much simpler, and cleaner cut, if we reformed the existing policies instead of imposing new ones.

If you carefully examined the mass of material that has been generated on President Carter's chosen instrument in the coal area, as I have had to do, you would have your doubts about additional regulation greatly reinforced. As you know, since 1977 he has been stressing forcing the conversion of electric power plants or large factories using oil and gas to coal or other alternative fuels.

Examination of the program indicates it provides rather sweeping authority to the Economic Regulatory Administration of the Department of Energy without providing adequate guidance about what policy procedures should be followed. The almost inevitable result of this will be the familiar one of excessive expenditures and very few results.

Now, these restrictions, of course, largely were inspired by sincere

11

concerns over the environment, coal mine worker health and safety, and energy monopoly. We cannot totally dismiss all these fears. What we can object to is the failure to admit candidly that these objectives conflict with the desire to increase coal use. At the very least, silence on the problem is further evidence of a general unwillingness to treat the issues forthrightly.

Moreover, the concern over competition in energy is highly inappropriate. The evidence suggests that competition in coal is vigorous and increasing. The Department of Justice has correctly argued that the major barrier is the coal leasing moratorium which prevents potential entrants into the coal industry from securing coal leases.

It can be further argued that the environmental movement has become too successful. The environmentalists are clearly obsessed with a fear that if they relent for an instant, they will be overwhelmed by an imagined irresistible power of industry. In fact, the best business has been able to do is to secure escape clause provisions or, worse, cooperate with the environmental movement when some parochial business interest could be served.

Once again we have produced an all too familiar result, of inadequate attainment of goals at excessive costs. Given these situations, it becomes appropriate seriously to consider radical reforms in the policies affecting coal and, of course, other energy resources. Again, the Carter program goes in the wrong direction. The energy board is another excessive grant of powers with an ill-defined mandate.

There are many alternatives one may suggest. The first, quite clearly, is a radical simplification of the mass of rules that are hindering the leasing of federal coal lands and, for that matter, federal energy resources of all types.

Secondly, we may seriously reconsider whether it was wise to have passed so stringent a Coal Mine Reclamation Act and, similarly, to have so vigorously enforced this law under the regulations.

Thirdly, we ought to reconsider several elements of the Clean Air Amendments of 1977. The prime target, obviously, at least to me, is the notorious Metzenbaum amendment, which protects local coal from displacement. This is an entirely extraneous and inappropriate intrusion into the environmental realm of parochial local economic interests.

Questions can seriously be raised about whether it was wise to embark on so ambitious a program of preventing significant deterioration; that is, imposing severe limits on the increase in air pollution in areas where it was deemed vital to prevent the serious deterioration of air quality. These areas may well have been much too broadly defined, and rules may have been much too stringent.

Last but not least in the coal area, it is not clear, given the extreme difficulties we have had in effectively implementing earlier regulations (1971) affecting pollution control at new electric power plants and factories, that we should have embarked on a new program of more stringent regulations affecting pollution control.

In general, then, it seems desirable to think very seriously about loosening the regulatory pressures on the coal industry. Otherwise, coal will be headed further in the same direction nuclear power has moved, of being constrained to a very severe degree by environmental and other government regulations.

More broadly, we should reconsider the whole package of restrictions on the development of coal, nuclear power, and other domestic energy resources. I fear we are heading for near paralysis of action in the energy realm. The consequences of this, whatever they may be, are likely to be far worse than anything we have experienced thus far.

4

MORRIS A. ADELMAN
Professor of Economics
Massachusetts Institute of Technology

Much of any energy policy hangs, so to speak, on the peg of the world oil market and what we expect there. It seems to me all that we can reasonably expect is that prices will rise further and the supply will remain unstable, with chronic shortages punctuated by occasional gluts.

This will be the case, regardless of what the United States imports or even regardless of world consumption. The less we consume, the less they are going to produce. The supply will be kept tight because the OPEC core of nations, the Persian Gulf countries, have planned it that way, and they have been able to execute their plans.

Now, the usual explanation for the last year's shortage and price gyrations is the Iranian cutback. But this cannot possibly be the explanation. The loss of the DC-10 represented about 12 to 15 percent of domestic air transportation capacity. The Iranian export cut was only about 4 percent of the total world market.

The chronic shortages since the Iranian revolution result from the manipulation of output by the Persian Gulf nations, chiefly by Saudi Arabia.

In January, in the middle of the month, Saudi output was cut abruptly from 10½ million to 8 million barrels a day. That was when rising spot prices exploded, because supply was so much less than the amount demanded. And once spot prices exploded, both in crude and products, that furnished the beacon for contract prices, or list prices, to be raised. The usual excuse was that the contract prices were, after all, simply following the market.

The agreement at Geneva, at the end of March and then at the end of June, simply codified the practice. I'll quote now from a trade journal: "They have trimmed supply in line with a partial restoration of Iranian production. The object of the cutbacks is to keep the market tight and let the pricing initiative remain with the OPEC members."

These Persian Gulf producers are fine-tuning a cartel and trying to match supply and demand at their prices. But they are doing this with blunt instruments. They don't know current consumption any more than anybody else does. Even the production numbers are a bit shaky these days. So it is a very clumsy kind of cartel. They must err, up or down, and, naturally enough, better a little down. They would much prefer that the market be tight than loose.

So, lower consumption will be no help in heading off this chronic shortage, because the less we consume, the less they produce. There will be, as there is now, a chronic contrived deficit. Prices will keep rising because the producing nations have not yet achieved the monopoly optimum price. How far up they can go, I don't know. Sheik Yamani has floated a price of $40, but how seriously, I don't know.

If anybody doubts that the picture I draw is valid he should look five years back. From 1973 to 1978, consumption in the OECD, as Professor Hogan has pointed out, rose only about 2 or 3 percent—not per year but for the whole five-year period. The demand for OPEC oil was down by about 3 percent. The realization of a stagnant market has finally sunk in. Two years ago, the CIA was predicting a demand on OPEC in 1985 of 49 million barrels a day. It is obvious, now, that the demand will be around 30 million, a little more, a little less.

That is why there was the drastic cutback in Saudi Arabian expansion plans. No more complex explanation is needed. The market is not there, so they are not building the capacity.

Yet, during this time of stagnant demand, since the end of 1973 after the price explosion, prices have trebled. That is nominal; in real terms, they have not much more than doubled.

The future, I think, will resemble the past, because the same factors are operating. It will be somewhat worse, harder going. Because these nations controlling the output are richer, they can better afford production cutbacks. Higher prices will get us more shortages and more serious ones.

14

Now, what can be done about this? The answer is, not very much. Lower oil imports, which seem to be the centerpiece of this administration's policy, will not get us lower prices, for reasons I have just explained.

There are many and vague and therefore powerful references to some kinds of political benefits, freedom of action in foreign affairs, or something. What this refers to is the threat of a very drastic cutback of supplies by the producing nations, so drastic as to cripple economic life here.

Whether we import 8½ million barrels daily, or reduce the amount to 4½ million, which nobody believes is possible, the threat still remains. Furthermore, if such a cutback takes place in the supplies of friendly nations, it is just as much a threat to us. Let imports rise or fall; there is no change in the political environment.

The real administration objective can be stated as follows, I think: We will, from a position of greater strength, have a deal, or even a partnership, with the OPEC nations. They need us, just as we need them, and so we will have an agreement for stable prices and reliable supplies. We will wrap up political and oil issues in one global package. That was Mr. Kissinger's ego trip, and Mr. Carter had launched on it even before his inauguration.

It is, however, an illusion. There is no basis for an agreement between consuming and producing nations. We can only make a bargain if we are free to give or not give something, and if the other party has something we want which he, too, is free to give or not give.

In point of fact, we have nothing to offer Saudi Arabia and its partners, and vice versa. We must give them military protection, regardless of what they do, and, hence, they need give us nothing for this; we have no bargaining power.

We cannot give or withhold technical assistance; they can buy it. If we give it to them free, then we are simply making a payment in kind; it is barter, just as wasteful and awkward as barter always is.

In return, they have nothing to give us. We should give them nothing in return for producing the quantity of oil which suits their interests to produce, because they will produce it anyway. Any promise they make of more supply or steady supply is, as the lawyers would say, void for vagueness. Worse yet, there is no way of enforcing it.

Agreements are enforced by competition or by law, or both. If somebody breaks his word, people have no more to do with him. He's out of business. But there is no competition in world oil today. A judge can tell the promise-breaker to pay up or go to jail, or have his bank account seized, but there is no law against the sovereign state.

The catalog or list of promises broken by Saudi Arabia is long. The trouble is not that they are worse than other people. They are just like everybody else. So, if there is no kind of sanction, competition, or law, they won't do what they promised.

There are two implications for policy in this look at oil imports. Usually, economists complicate life; in this case, I think economic reasoning simplifies it in both the political and the economic domain.

In the political domain, in Southern Africa or the Middle East, this nation ought to do what seems best and not be distracted by vain hopes of buying lower prices or assured supply. We cannot buy the suppliers, or, rather, they won't stay bought.

In the economic domain, imports are worth cutting back only if they save money. And money, of course, is nothing but a way of reckoning up capital and labor. Imports, then, are worth cutting back only if they save capital and labor; they are not worth cutting back for their own sake and in spite of the possible cost.

What can be done, perhaps, to some limited extent, is to provide security against short-term reductions, and that is what the strategic reserve is supposed to be doing. Also, it may be advisable—but this is a more debatable point—since higher prices are coming anyway, to anticipate them and put a tariff or tax on the consumption of oil products.

The auto mileage requirements are really a tax on driving, but they are acceptable because they don't look like a tax.

Now, a word or two on the Carter program. The best appraisal of it, perhaps, is in the fact that the OPEC nations, in June, changed prices and adjourned without even waiting for the Tokyo Summit. They had taken our measure and knew they needed to pay it no attention.

I won't comment on the various energy-saving measures. I think they are adequately covered already. I will just comment on the proposed quotas on oil imports. The 1977 cap, which is 8.8 million barrels daily gross, and 8.5 net, is an easy target. In fact, there is a pretty fair chance that, even if nothing is done, we will never get up that high again.

Now, if the quotas do bite, then that will force up the domestic price, as has already been remarked. It will also tend to force up the world price. The reason is—and excuse me for making a technical point here—that they cause a section of the demand curve, confronting the sellers, to be absolutely inelastic. That is to say, over the interval between what the sellers would sell, without a quota, and the amount that they are permitted to sell in the United States, there is no relation between price and the amount demanded. They can, with impunity, raise the price and not lose anything in the way of sales because they have lost it already. Therefore, a quota—a quota that bites—will not only not reduce the world price, but it will actually, if anything, raise it. And, as has already been remarked, fitting it into the price control scheme is a fresh and almost unbearable complication.

5

EDWARD J. MITCHELL
Professor of Business Economics
University of Michigan
Director, Energy Policy Studies
American Enterprise Institute

President Carter's policy, described by him as an import reduction program, is primarily a response to the symptoms of the Iranian cut-off and Saudi Arabian cut-back in supply, namely, the long gas lines and the higher prices.

This response is hardly novel. It is exactly the kind of response that President Nixon made when, as a result of the Arab embargo, we found ourselves facing the same symptoms.

The logic of the approach is that of insulating ourselves from OPEC and the world oil market. President Nixon called it "energy independence"; President Carter calls it "import reduction," I think, reflecting the diminished gullibility of the public, but the logic is essentially the same.

Import reduction, per se, does not contribute to the national security or reliability of supply, at least unless these imports are replaced by domestic supply. And that is not likely to happen under a quota, under the current environment, in this country. I am assuming now that the quota is binding; otherwise the quota is meaningless. At the present time, the numbers cited by President Carter are not binding, but we have to assume that, if he is serious about this policy, at some point they will be binding.

The reason why oil imports will not be displaced by domestic supply is that the only mechanism that a quota has for bringing about increased domestic supply is increasing the domestic price. We reduce the total supply to the domestic market; therefore, the price goes up, and therefore, domestic supply increases. Right now, that would not happen at all because we have price controls on oil and price controls on natural gas, and those are the obvious places, at least in the intermediate term, where the supply response would come from.

What would we get if, for example, a quota cut back oil imports by a million barrels per day as opposed to what they would otherwise be? All we would get is a million barrels per day domestic shortage of oil.

Down the road, if we ever do deregulate oil, as we are supposed to do in 1981, then the price could rise. But if the windfall profits tax is put on, as expected, that will take most of the supply incentive away from those price increases, and the whole burden of adjusting to the quota and the limited imports will be borne by higher prices inducing less consumption.

The gist of all this is that, in effect, a quota replaces the risk of a shortage, or the risk of a price increase, with the certainty of a shortage, or the certainty of a price increase. And, by analogy, it is equivalent to avoiding the risk of war by surrendering to the enemy.

I conclude, at this time, there would be no significant reliability or national security benefits from installing a quota.

My second point, with regard to the quota, is the same one that Professor Adelman just made. Rather than reducing the demand for world oil, as one might imagine that it would, it does not really reduce the demand; it changes the shape of the demand curve. What it says is: we will buy this much oil abroad, no more, no less. If you reduce your price, we are not going to buy any more. And what seller would reduce his price if he didn't think he was going to get a substantial increase in sales?

By the same token, a reduced quantity of imports could be achieved either by a price increase or by this so-called quota. If the quota is installed and imports actually fall, then OPEC, by raising its price to the level that would have induced those smaller amounts of imports without a quota, would not reduce its sales. Therefore, it has every incentive to increase the price in response to a binding quota.

Compare the quota with a tariff, which is an alternative instrument. The tariff does have some positive effects. First, the tariff really does decrease the demand for OPEC oil in a meaningful way, as economists use the term "reduction in demand." It has the effect, therefore, of tending to depress the optimal price that OPEC might set. It induces lower world prices.

The result is that tariff revenues, which would otherwise go to OPEC nations in the form of their export tariffs, would, instead accrue to our treasury rather than to their treasury. Thus, there are positive benefits from the point of view of reducing the cost of acquiring oil from going to a tariff. There are no such benefits from going to a quota; indeed, the reverse is true.

Neither a quota nor a tariff will give us any reliability or national security benefits unless there is some displacement of the imports with domestic supply, and that will not happen unless there is domestic decontrol.

Now, the question is: Why, then, is there a bias in the political system for choosing quotas? The fact is that, since World War II, most of the time we have had quotas of one kind or another on the importation of oil. And, in fact, for fourteen years, from 1959 to 1973, we had a very elaborate oil import control program.

The first reason, I believe, for the belief in quotas rather than tariffs, is that the price increase, which will inevitably follow the installation of a binding quota, both at home and abroad, will not be directly attributable, in the minds of the public, to the actions of the President. It will be the domestic oil companies and OPEC that will raise the price. In the case of a tariff, it is rather obvious that the price is going up just simply because we are adding a tariff onto the existing price of oil.

Another reason why the political system chooses quotas and, in particular, why the political system will keep a quota, once it has it, is that as in the Mandatory Oil Import Program, spanning the Eisenhower to the Nixon years, these valuable import rights are allocated on a primarily political basis to favored groups. These import rights are nothing more than the equivalent of money, and, in effect, political favor can be purchased by them. It was for that reason that the oil import program lasted as long as it did. I spent three years on the oil policy committee in the government dishing out these import licenses, and I can testify that the basis for their distribution was not economic.

Finally, I think the reason why quotas are chosen goes back, in some way, to the "gapological" approach—a term I coined some five or six years ago. This is the notion that at some point in the study of energy, someone discovered that barrels could be counted, and that consumption equaled domestic supply plus imports. Since then, policy makers, mesmerized by that equation, have felt that any worthwhile policy has to play somehow upon those numbers.

I would make one final point. Many of the disadvantages that come from quotas would also come from mandatory types of conservation. They would, as Professor Adelman mentioned, tend to make our demand curve for oil and energy more inelastic, and when you make it inelastic, you make it more attractive for a monopoly supplier to raise his price.

19

6.
Questions and Answers

Q: Given your criticisms of the President's program, what would you gentlemen have had him do? It would seem that you have issued cautions on the synfuels programs, cautions on the quotas or the conservation part, and criticisms of the coal policy, so what would you have him do?

PROFESSOR MITCHELL: The first thing that should be done is to decontrol oil and gas prices, so that we do get some increase in domestic supply, not ten, or twenty, or thirty years from now, but in the nearer term. And, secondly, place a significant tariff on oil imports for the reasons that I just gave.

An energy policy, built on those two things, decontrol and a tariff, it seems to me, takes care of most of the issues that confront us.

Q: And you think the synfuels investment is just a great mistake?

PROFESSOR MITCHELL: If we have a tariff the synfuels investment will occur if the cost of the synfuels is less than the OPEC price, plus the tariff. If they cost more than that, the synfuels investment won't take place.

The problem is choosing the size of the tariff. It is not easy to say how many dollars per barrel a tariff should be. But all these other problems take care of themselves, once the domestic price level is where we want it to be.

Q: On that same point, what about the windfall profits tax and the impact it would have on domestic production?

PROFESSOR MITCHELL: In concept, I disagree with the windfall profits tax, both from an equity point of view and certainly from an efficiency point of view. From an efficiency point of view, it is clear that the windfall profits tax makes matters worse. It is harmful to the economy. From an equity point of view, the federal government will get half the profits to begin with, plus whatever it can get from bonuses on federal lands, and royalties. I don't perceive the powerful equity concerns that other people have.

There will be a forthcoming publication in our AEI energy series, which will deal specifically with the equity and efficiency aspects of decontrol and windfalls.

20

PROFESSOR GORDON: Two things came to mind as I sat here. I was struck by something about the President's policy we haven't said yet—that all his proposals have the characteristic of postponing things. They are ostensible decisions rather than real decisions. Many of these actions may never be taken. The synfuels program, for example, looks to be the liquid-metal, fast-breeder reactor of the 1980s.

More broadly, as I tried to suggest and now want to emphasize more strongly, the problem is not just price controls. It is an assortment of controls—not only at the federal but at the state and local levels that is hampering energy development in this country. We have to seriously reconsider whether we want so complicated a set of regulations.

I would very vigorously criticize Mr. Carter for never once forthrightly admitting that this is a problem and never being willing to consider it seriously. Long after that famous sixty-day period in which we were going to get the word on how to improve our coal situation, we have Mr. Schlesinger's suggestions in this area still sitting in the Office of Management and Budget.

DR. RUSSELL: I would comment on that first question about what else to do. First of all, I would go along with Professor Mitchell's comments on decontrol and on a tariff.

A synfuels program, of a very different sort than the President is aiming at, seems to make some sense to me. That would be a synfuels program aimed at information about what the long-run costs of some of these installations will be.

Such a synfuels program would include, it seems to me, putting one, or two, or three of these commercial-sized plants into place. The reason for that is, much of the information that is required is socioeconomic information, and that information cannot be obtained without actually putting steel and concrete on the ground and seeing what actually happens.

The third point I would make is that the strategic storage program is the key issue. The key problems are those short-run interruptions of supply. As Professor Adelman suggested earlier, the only way we can deal with that—and not deal with it terribly well, even so—is through some ability to restrict the immediate effects of disruptions of supply on security.

Consequently, I would think a strategic storage program—probably very different from the one we have now, emphasizing private storage and available storage capacity, rather than grounds-up storage capacity—should be urged at a very rapid rate, even at times when world oil markets are tight. The tightness of those world oil markets—again, as Professor Adelman suggested—is a function of decisions outside. It will not be affected by a few more barrels of imports.

The fourth thing I think the President should do, or could do, would be to find some way to separate out the energy problem from the social problem, from the poverty problem, in this country. It has been these equity issues—this fear of how the poor manage to get to work and to heat their homes—which has been driving energy policy and driving it, for the most part, in the wrong direction.

We need to concern ourselves about these issues of social equity, but we should try to separate them from energy in some fashion. What that fashion might be is very difficult to suggest, but, certainly, it means something like general programs of support rather than energy-associated programs of support.

Q: Where would you get the money for that? The idea of the windfall profits tax, I think, is to make some money available for these purposes.

PROFESSOR MITCHELL: Where do we get the money for all of the other things we, in this society, feel it is useful to do? The fact is, we get it from our tax system. It may well be that the tariff on imported oil might be a source of those funds, but it is better that this be drawn from general government revenues.

Q: Professor Mitchell, you suggested, by implication, at least, that there would be a very large supply response from decontrol and the absence of a windfall profits tax that would reduce imports over time. How large a supply response do you think would be forthcoming from that approach?

PROFESSOR MITCHELL: If I seemed to imply that, I didn't mean to imply that. I have no estimate; I have no model of how much domestic supplies will increase if the price rises. I only know that they will be higher if the price increases and if there is no windfall profits tax, and that there is no hope, in the short term, of getting supplies from anywhere else.

If it turns out that we just don't have any more oil and gas, which I seriously doubt, other than what would come under the President's program we will discover that. But, in either event, this is information that we don't know, that no econometric model can tell us, that we will only know if we, in fact, decontrol.

Q: Then, it is quite possible there could be no increase or very little increase in production under decontrol as far as you are concerned?

PROFESSOR MITCHELL: It is possible, but I think not likely. If we look at the past, we see that higher prices imply more drilling and more discoveries, and qualitatively, the relationship is there.

All I am suggesting is we would be operating in a zone in which we have never operated before. I think it is presumptuous of people to say that the elasticity of supply, from $15 to $25 per barrel, is going to be 0.5 or whatever. I don't know what it is, and I don't think that the policy should hinge on the elasticity being some particular number.

Q: Professor Mitchell, I am having difficulty understanding the advangages of the tariff and what it would do in terms of inflation. Could you speak to that?

PROFESSOR MITCHELL: The tariff has the effect that it does reduce demand for oil in the world market, and whether it is monopolized or competitive, a reduction in demand implies a lower price. That is, it is at least optimal from the point of view of the seller to lower his price, and that implies a transfer of wealth from OPEC treasuries to the U.S. Treasury. That is the fundamental positive effect of a tariff.

On the other side, the domestic price would rise, because presumably, OPEC would not reduce its price by the amount of the tariff, and that would result in some additional domestic supplies. As a result, there would be some increased reliability of supply. I would also endorse what Dr. Russell said, that there certainly are other methods of increasing reliability.

PROFESSOR ADELMAN: I wonder if I could say something about a tariff. I agree with what Professor Mitchell has said. I would go a bit further.

One point is that an obstacle to it is the reluctance of any individual nation to raise its own energy costs above the costs of nations with whom it competes on the world market. Therefore, the chances of an effective tariff are much greater if all of the OECD nations do this together. The chances of them doing it together, as things are today, are not very great.

The second point about a tariff sounds like a technical point, but I think it is rather important. We are much better off with an ad valorem tariff such that every time the world price is raised, the amount of tariff goes up proportionately or even disproportionately. Then, the exporting nations are on notice that the price response on the part of consumers will be a great deal more than would result simply from their own actions. Consumers get hit with the higher prices, but we can make them whole if we collect a large part of the revenues at home.

Indeed, an ad valorem tariff can be used as a tool to get a great deal and, at the limit, even all of the OPEC revenues back in our own pockets. The OPEC nations have always been quite sensitive to consuming country taxes. They have protested them, and I think they show a sound instinct in doing so.

The consuming countries may drift in this direction in trying to hold down consumption by means of product taxes or tariffs. This is where we may gravitate in the next decade.

Q: Professor Adelman, I still don't understand why the producers would lower their prices if there were a tariff. Why would they cut their prices just because we would add a tariff every time they increased prices?

PROFESSOR ADELMAN: They won't necessarily reduce their prices. I think both Professor Mitchell and I are assuming—or at least I will do it explicitly—that as they raise prices there comes a point where they are at their optimum. That is the farthest north they can go.

If they raise the price farther, they will lose so much business that they lose money, and then they won't want to raise the price any more. At that point, if you levy a tariff, it means that either they lose business and lose profits, or they reduce the price and don't lose as much. If you credit them with ordinary business sense, I think that is what they will do.

DR. RUSSELL: Could I add a point to that? As they lose business, even if they are not at that point where the OPEC cartel, as a whole, is at its optimal price, it becomes more and more difficult for the cartel to decide which country is going to produce how much. And it makes it more difficult for them to, in fact, reduce production overall. Consequently, lower demand tends to reduce their ability to control supplies and, therefore, hold the price up.

PROFESSOR ADELMAN: I agree with that, and I would add one point. If the tariff is an ad valorem tariff, it means that any reduction of price gives the price-reducing seller a disproportionate advantage, because some of the tariff, in effect, is rebated to him or to the buyer. And so it gives sellers an inducement to lower the price to get more business.

Q: Give us your analysis of what would happen if the world buying nations, starting with this country, were to go to a sealed bidding

24

system, where we buy and try to conceal the price that we are buying at, in order to encourage some competition among the sellers.

PROFESSOR ADELMAN: That was a proposal I made some years ago, and that was a nonbinding quota. I think it would have worked three years ago when I first published it, or six years ago when I first proposed it. I think it would even have worked a year ago.

I am not at all sure it would work today. I think it is worth doing, because there is nothing lost thereby, but it is obviously not in the cards.

Q: Why not? Why isn't it something we should be pushing harder?

PROFESSOR ADELMAN: Well, maybe we should be, but I would say it is the last thing that the administration wants. It is very keen on keeping good relations with what it calls "our close friends in OPEC." One of those friends is gone, so we cling even more tightly to the other.

This is a fixed dogma in foreign policy and oil policy. I won't try to explain it. I don't have any expertise in psychology.

Q: Could I ask a question about the synfuels program? One of the arguments for the proposed benefits of synfuel is that prices may be higher for synfuel products than for OPEC oil, but they won't be that much higher.

There is also an argument that the comparison should be made in actual production costs rather than prices. Production costs in OPEC nations might be a fiftieth or less of synfuels production costs. Could somebody comment on that, whether that is a correct assumption, and what the implications would be for cartel actions in the event we do have a synfuel industry producing high cost products?

DR. RUSSELL: There are two comments that could be made. First of all, it is certainly true that production costs are going to be considerably lower for OPEC oil than for synfuels. Therefore, if we were optimizing the world use of resources, and seeking to maximize the per capita income of the world, it would make absolutely no sense to produce synfuels when conventional oil could be produced more cheaply.

Of course, we are not concerned with the per capita income of the world. We are concerned more with the per capita income of the United States. Consequently, we are not optimizing on a world level, but we are optimizing within the United States. This means that the appropriate comparison would be between the cost of imported oil and the cost of the synthetic oil—if what we are looking at is the United States alone.

The second response is that, clearly, OPEC countries, if they formed an effective cartel, could in the future manipulate the price of oil.

They could reduce the price of oil and make the synfuels plants, which appear uneconomic at the monopoly price of oil charged by OPEC, appear even less economic later. And that is an uncertainty which may be hindering private enterprise in entering a synthetic fuels program.

Now, that was a serious concern, I think, three or five years ago, at the time of the Ford and Nixon administrations. It was a serious cause for saying we needed to provide a floor price for oil in order to encourage domestic production. There are not many people now who would infer, I think, from OPEC behavior, that OPEC is willing to reduce price significantly in order to punish, let us say, the very small quantities of high cost synthetic fuels that are likely to come on the market in the next few years.

But the uncertainty about OPEC manipulation does provide some argument for government action through instruments such as purchase guarantees which would eliminate the uncertainty that someday OPEC countries, for reasons of their own, would seek to undercut synthetic fuels plants and try to drive them out of business, only to raise the price again later.

Q: Could the President raise tariffs at this time, when we are entering into a trade agreement designed to lower tariffs over the years to come? Would it be a violation of the Tokyo rounds?

PROFESSOR ADELMAN: I don't know. I shouldn't answer very confidently, but maybe that would be an additional reason for what I said before, that this will more likely be done by all the nations together, or most of them, rather than by one at a time. Can anybody answer that?

PROFESSOR MITCHELL: The president, acting alone, can install a tariff based on the same law that enables him to install a quota without the consent of Congress.

President Ford did that, and began to install a tariff, first $1 per barrel, then $2 per barrel, and then he eventually backed off, because of the political heat from the Congress. But that case was not taken all the way up to the Supreme Court, so we do not know whether the president could, under the national security part of the Trade Expansion Act of 1953, install a tariff as opposed to a quota.

My guess would be that he could. It is a means of restricting imports just as a quota is. Therefore, the president, acting alone, could install the tariff.

DR. RUSSELL: There is, in fact, a fee on oil imports now, and what would be involved would be to simply increase that fee. And that authority does, as I understand, exist.

PROFESSOR GORDON: In regard to the broader implications, I don't think we have significant trade agreements with the OPEC countries. Our trade agreements are mostly with countries that produce goods comparable to our own, so that this would not interfere greatly with the General Agreement on Tariffs and Trade framework.

Q: The Geological Survey estimates there are from 50 to 127 billion barrels of crude oil, plus natural gas in huge quantities, still in this country and offshore, producible by conventional means. Nobody ever seems to say much about getting more of this. We have gone now to synthetic fuels at a tremendously high cost. Is there any thought given to getting more of this energy? It would take a lot more to produce it, a lot of it is marginal, and some is undiscovered, but it is supposed to be there. There is a 95 percent chance that there is 50 billion barrels.

Could any of you address yourselves to that kind of a program?

PROFESSOR ADELMAN: Well, a number of us have been thinking about it. I would join Ed Mitchell in saying we simply do not know how much of it would be forthcoming at what price. I don't think there is any question there could be more than at present. How much more, we can't say.

For a minute I thought you were talking about something else— not undiscovered oil, but discovered oil that has not been brought out on the first or second pass. Enhanced oil recovery is, in a way, just like synfuels. We need a lot more technology and know-how than we have now. But it can be put into practice a lot more quickly in very small bites in many places, and at much less expense, than synfuel production can.

We do not know how much we will get out, when we transfer methods that look good in the laboratory to the field. But neither do we know how much we will get out of synfuels. I don't think there can be any question that we will get a great deal more for our money from enhanced oil recovery than from synfuels.

PROFESSOR GORDON: But, of course, we have already given the basic answer, which is decontrol. We don't need to do much more than decontrol to get these sorts of things done. It may also be necessary, radically, to change our oil and gas leasing policies.

27

DR. RUSSELL: There is one other point that perhaps could be made. It is not necessarily, as economists say, moving *up* the supply curve that is required—that is to say, higher prices. But it is possibly also *shifting* the supply curve to the right, and let me explain.

The uncertainties that have been created by the price control programs and the distortions that have been created by the different regulations that exist have almost certainly caused oil companies to produce less at each price, than they would have been producing without the regulations and without the uncertainties.

So, it need not mean that higher prices alone will be required to generate additional conventional oil and gas production. Reduction of the uncertainties and reduction of some of the regulatory problems would cause more to be produced even at the same price than has been produced before.

Q: I wanted to go back to your gloomy assessment of the world oil market and OPEC. Given the internal needs of each of the OPEC countries, even Saudi Arabia, isn't there some level of cash they need to generate? Isn't there some minimum production level below which OPEC has great trouble reducing production to try to prop up a price?

What level is that? Is there any way the United States—alone or working with OECD nations—could so reduce its demand for oil that it would push OPEC to that point? And if we couldn't push beyond it, could we at least would ensure ourselves increased stability of supply?

PROFESSOR ADELMAN: That floor exists, but nobody knows where it is. It is the kind of question, of course, that those countries don't want to find out the answer to.

The trouble is that the floor is subject to a rising tendency and also a falling tendency. The rising tendency is the marvelous adaptability of the human race in getting used to spending a lot more money in a short time. And the OPEC nations have amazed the world at their ability to spend amounts that were undreamed of just a few years ago.

I don't think anybody guessed right on that, and most of us guessed far, far too low, so the floor tends to rise. But with the increases in price, the floor can still go down, because fewer barrels bring in a lot more money.

Now, to say where and when these two will offset each other depends, ultimately, on what I said before, How far can the price be raised before getting to, and passing, monopoly heaven, namely, where revenues are at a maximum? Then higher prices will lose revenues.

A number of people made guesses, and some fairly elaborate

models were constructed. Now they don't look very good. And those of us who admitted from the start that we were ignorant of where heaven was—just like astronomers who have never been able to find it—don't have to apologize for yet another mistake. [Laughter.]

PROFESSOR HOGAN: We can search for that floor and, if we want to, for the very stable production level, by imposing the tariff. We can make the tariff larger and larger to drive down the price and the demand for OPEC oil until they have to maintain a certain level of production.

But it is probably not in our own interest to do that, and that is the important point. The tariff would impose cost on many domestic consumers, and it would reduce the efficiency for many of our production processes. We don't want to make that tariff larger than would be the equivalent cost of the imported oil, the marginal imported oil, with the security and economic problems we have talked about. It follows logically, then, that some instability in supply, some possibilities of disruptions, will have to be absorbed in the future. That's what makes the strategic reserve so important. The strategic reserve is something we ought to take on as a much more important policy objective, possibly while we search for the optimum level of the tariff.

We are stating implicitly—or explicitly in a fact sheet from the White House—that we believe imported oil probably costs $15 or $20 a barrel more than we are paying for it. That is certainly the message we get from the synthetic fuels program. But if we imposed that kind of tariff on oil, the political process would reverse the judgment about how much that imported oil really costs. That is the step that we ought to make so that we can make the debate, the very political debate, explicit. Then all of us can vote on what we think imported oil really does cost us.